To Cl...

Holly Magill

Thank you
– hope you
enjoy

The Becoming of
Lady Flambé

[signature]

2018
Oct

Indigo Dreams Publishing

First Edition: The Becoming of Lady Flambé
First published in Great Britain in 2018 by:
Indigo Dreams Publishing
24, Forest Houses
Cookworthy Moor
Halwill
Beaworthy
Devon
EX21 5UU

www.indigodreams.co.uk

ISBN 978-1-910834-86-2

British Library Cataloguing in Publication Data. A CIP record for this book can be obtained from the British Library.

Designed and typeset in Palatino Linotype by Indigo Dreams.
Cover design by Ronnie Goodyer at Indigo Dreams
Printed and bound in Great Britain by 4edge Ltd.

Papers used by Indigo Dreams are recyclable products made from wood grown in sustainable forests following the guidance of the Forest Stewardship Council.

For all the families –
especially the families who didn't necessarily realise they were.

Acknowledgements

Massive thank yous are due to all my friends, near and far, writers and non-writers alike, who've been there for tea, wine, venting, and laughter; Mum for driving me to north Wales and back in a day on an emergency laptop run, and for generally being awesome; Kate Garrett, editor of Picaroon and Three Drops from a Cauldron, where two of these poems were first published; Prosperity Chinese restaurant, Rhuddlan, where the idea of a woman performing with flaming bananas first popped into my head over a potentially fatal dessert; Brett Evans for putting up with me banging on about said woman and furnishing me with many further puddings.

The Becoming of Lady Flambé is Holly Magill's debut collection.

CONTENTS

'I never asked to be born –
shit happens.'
                    Flambé

(Wayne)
New arrivals

Tuesday I took custody of my most valuable possession;
his name is Steve and he is a three year old
Asian elephant.

It was a long journey to the agreed drop-off – forgive me
if I don't specify the location – and then back to camp;
stressful, the constant worry that the paperwork would be…
that unforeseen difficulties would derail the operation.
I've waited for this – will finally set me apart

from those spit-and-sawdust outfits, glorified petting
parlours with added glittered-up tarts – God knows
we've enough of those.

The "homecoming" is inauspicious,
the engine grumbling to nothing; no matter –
the grand reveal will be… Exceptional.

My precious cargo sleeps his wrinkle-skinned sleep;
big, clumsy body nestled warm in cushioning straw –
motorways and A roads are tolerable, but further out
is all potholes, ruts – it's not safe.

Camp is lit up for such a late hour, an orange glow
gathered like a net of open eyes to the one plot
that guarantees trouble:

a purple camper van painted with freewheeling
silver ballerinas – self-indulgence. She is half-lit
in its doorway, face even more masked
than her freakdom normally has it.

Muffled bumping behind me from the container;

Steve is awake – I need to get back, soothe him.
But the woman's eyes

seethe in the dark, will not let me

turn away. She waits
for me to draw near, much nearer
than I'd like, before she lets me
see the thing she cradles.

She had it, *Bella says.* And this one stays.

My earliest memory

A big grey bum is reversing
towards me, like the lorries at Tesco,
but without the beeping noises.

I'm little – pee down my legs
into my frilled white socks.

The Girls – arms jittery now they're
unstrung from trapezes and ponies –
smoke and slouch by their trailer.

A normal kid would run.

A normal kid would shout *Mummy!*
Shout *Daddy!* And parents

would come scoop her up from the dirt.

A normal kid would scream
when her right foot is stomped
by an elephant.

Someone says he is *three whole tonnes!*

One of The Girls, high-rise blonde hair,
swallows her chewing gum, bends double
coughing, tears ploughing her make-up.

My ambulance is a purple van
painted with silver twirling angels,
all their feet are pointy.

No sirens or flashing blue lights.
Traffic is bad.

(Bella and Jolly-Boy wait)
Every family is different

The woman with the – get this! – actual beard
and the guy with the over-plucked eyebrows
sit in the far corner of the waiting area.

Her tiny feet are crossed, elbows tucked,
vintage white satin coat – Chanel?
That bloodstain's not going to come out.

His hands work compulsively, shaping
miniature creatures from pages ripped
out of our old magazines.

Some of us loiter at the desk; knowing,
as nurses especially, we shouldn't

stare. But the paper animals are really cool;
a longer and longer procession marches
the coffee table's rim as the clock
limps the hours by.

Lions and tigers roar their jaws to the ceiling;
monkeys wiggle their bums, bears beat bongos,
ponies with braided tails and flying legs dance.

A little boy with a bandaged arm
tugs at his mum's sleeve.

Look Mum – the man's made all the animals!
Are you doing an elephant, Mister? You have to
do an elephant.

The man's hands fist and shake in his lap;
the woman, her with the actual, like, beard,
unfolds them, her ringed, white fingers
freeing a crushed pony made of OK!

If I am quiet, they'll let me stay

Let her in if she don't stink of elephant shit.

The Pony Girls' trailer is fugged
with Impulse and Silk Cut. Sequinned bottoms
and dirty jokes bounce high over my head.

In around their knees and spiky shoes,
I try not to drag my foot. Make myself
useful – pick up clods of cotton wool,
knickers, rinse their tights.

Kelly has huge hair – she needs 67 pins
for every performance – I've counted –
She's His favourite, everyone says it,
but in whispers.

Saturday she took me into town – just us:
Keep quiet and hold my hand. Good kid.
Later a big bottle of banana shampoo
came out of my backpack.
Ta-da! Magic!

She's my favourite too. I don't say it at all.

When they forget me, The Girls say more.
*Little lame-foot, what'll become…
even a ginger.*
They rhyme it with *finger.*

I learn to paint their toenails,
glue glitter-stars on hard to reach parts;
someone teaches me gold thread sewing.
She'll need skills if she's to be kept…

After every show, Kelly is cut-puppet limp;
skin clammy, happy make-up all gone,
her shiny slithered off.

If I'm still awake – and usually I am –
I unpin the big blonde Swiss roll
at the back of her head. Brush the spray
from the rough snakes, twine the curls
in my fingers. She goes sleepy.

Those times are my very best thing,
when the other Girls have gone
dancing in nightclubs, or to drink
in the nearest, cheapest pubs
and it's just me and Kelly,

'til the night I see

through the banana shampoo smell,
the sweat steaming up from her parting,
the blonde-stop:
red, red, red at her roots.

Actually, it's ginger.
I should know.

(Bella)
Why you are with us

I always hoped she would take to you more,
that in time the maternal instinct cruelly
constant in my useless form would hopscotch
across to her like head-lice in the summer.
(No matter what people say, they do prefer
clean hair to lay their eggs.)

She accused me – of course she did – of wanting
you for my own. Said she would never allow it,
she'd dump you on the nearest Social Services
herself if she ever caught me

lullaby-ing you to sleep, combing tangles
from your roaring russet hair or palming
you little packets of Cadbury's Buttons
when you look sad.

Then the text, two weeks after she went
to Ibiza: stayin. keep her if u want

A whole lot of horse tranquilizers

Who would do such a thing? people gasp,
One of God's great creatures – it's murder!

No one will tell what they do with Steve's body;
would need an enormous hole to bury it,
like a crater on the moon.

There's jokes about an almighty hog-roast,
only not a hog – I'm going vegetarian.

We don't see The Ring Master for days;
empties fly from the windows of his trailer,
glass tears shatter on the hard-standing.

My ruined foot tingles. Wasn't me
that did it – but I wish I had.

On the third evening, a portable CD player magics
up on his front step, blaring and distorted.

*Nellie the elephant packed her trunk
and said goodbye...*

In the folds of night across the way,
I press repeat on the remote
over and over.

Things I learn

Juggling – Jolly-Boy teaches me.
(Unicycling was a bit of a stretch.)

How to mix The Girls' fave drinks:
cheeky Vimtos and vodka limes,
at least six things with Malibu.

Avoid reversing elephants.

Juggling doesn't get you friends
at new schools. No one likes
a smart-arse.

How to – almost – be deaf
to yells of *'Pikey'* and *'Gyppo'*
and *'Cripple'*.

Violet-satin eye-shadow is really pretty
on other girls.

Always smile at Social Workers;
it's not their fault.

Multi-tasking is easy – I can juggle and cry
at the same time, even in the dark.

Never, ever call The Ring Master *Dad*.

(Jolly-Boy)
I'm mad, me

That's what people say, isn't it? The over-friendly
pub bore with 101 jokes for every captive barmaid;
women who refer to themselves as Bubbly,
squealing how Fat! and Ugly! their mates are;
men in Roadrunner ties, who live with their mums,
collect Dr. Who memorabilia, and who've never
got round to shedding their virginity.

Yes, I have double standards – there is much to snigger
at in a bloke who paints his skin white and scarlet to sweat
and fool at the centre of a half empty tent every night,
twice on Saturdays, Sundays and Bank Holidays.

There is much to amuse, but I've forgotten how to find
fun in the burn of the lights and see only glib boredom
on the kids' faces – they'd rather be chasing Pokémon.

Johnson's Baby wipes my face out afterwards;
I step out of the oversized orange shoes that squeak,
unpeel polka-dot pantaloons from legs mottling
to middle-aged creaks.

The shower's spittle-stream sluices me away
with the perspiration – I evaporate
with the steam on the mirror until

I am gone and the voices
can only cackle at nothing.

I'm mad, me.

We've been nowhere long enough
to see a doctor – and I cope – still

got a few pills kept back.
Some midnights I count them out
into my left palm. Razorblades in my right.

Firestarter

I'm guessing most girls don't get their first kiss
with a lad who eats fire seven nights a week,
and two matinees at weekends.

Close up he smells of spent match-tips;
I suck in the heat from his furnace-mouth,
combustion in my tits and belly.

I want him to roar me to nothing.

Want one? I hold out my cigarettes – after –
cos turns out one first can lead to another
once the spark catches.

And somehow he is the only guy around here
who doesn't smoke.

Damp squib
(on leaving)

The woman who gave birth to me left before
I worked out I could have a view on that.

The man who loosed sperm in her slipped
away in all but his physical presence.

Now you – first boy, first kiss, first fuck
– don't look like that cos I said *fuck*.

This cabaret in Blackpool – they want you
and your *sensational* fire-eating mouth.

What is it? You want tears?
I'm to beg you to stay?

Nah.

Ok, so it's not the Tower Ballroom,
but very, very near; might get to party
with the stars of *Strictly*.

Go. You'd be a twat not to.

Just one thing, I'd like to keep
your accelerant as a souvenir
of, well, us.

Told you from the start I'm weird.

Mystic Maureen chooses Ovaltine

Come inside if you must, but be gentle – look
how that curtain is fraying.

There are no leaves here to read for you, little one,
no china cups to swirl and upend.

I gave the tea set to Oxfam in Barnsley;
no good handing it on to the next
generation – they're all as fake
as I'd wish to be.

It's got a hold of me, you see, this malted beast;
addiction is only pretty in the young.

My fix is from the Co-op – I stock up
when it's BOGOF – best served in chunky mugs
I can hug my fingers round. The aches are terrible.

Caribbean heat should help with that;
always fancied a cruise. Every day
will be exactly the same.

So, no, I cannot read your destiny now, girl,
but sit with me here whilst my last candle soots
up these old chenille drapes and we'll drain
our drinks to the sludge at the bottom.

I am tired, I don't want to see anything more.

But perhaps you will.

No one tells me not to

We don't stay anywhere long, but I find
it's long enough to find boys and I get
good at eyeing them, fingering

the rim of my glass, making them
wonder if I'm the sort of girl who might –
and I find I'm the sort of girl who does.

I get none of the hassle normal
girls have to squirm around.

Be home by ten, or else. Careful
who you talk to. Don't let men buy
you drinks and you mustn't get into
anyone's car. Always make sure
we know where you are.

Get back to your room, no daughter of mine…

I go out Looking Like That.

And I fucking love it.

A small matter

The summer I turn sixteen, Jolly-Boy has a breakdown:
so sad – the kindest and least scary of all the clowns.

The Ring Master replaces him
with a talkative Welshman called Leon,
who throws knives in rhythm with 1950s jive.

Under scornful starlight, he tells me I'm *Special*
and licks already wet lips. A bouquet of blades flourish
from one hand, a signed photo – of himself – from the other.

I've no clue who he is.

Backstage he eyes my built-up boot – thinks me
oblivious. My spine tenses as his breath matches
the uneven roll of my hips at each step.

He'll take me on as his wife, he promises
The Ring Master – a deal done behind red curtains,
used notes and gentlemen's agreements. Unlucky

he has to part ways with the troupe
halfway across Norfolk. I'm not allowed

to throw knives after that. Even so, a man can function
with only one ear, and a missing testicle is a small matter.

Bella sees

Kelly had habitually subsisted purely
on vodka, chicken Pot Noodle, and Silk Cut.

But once morning – and noon and night –
sickness passed, she craved

bananas, consuming them by the bunch,
a trail of pungent yellow skins
wherever she went.

I would have named you Darcey or Margot,
but was overruled – it was for the best;
you were no more bound
for Covent Garden than I'd been.

Now you have your mother's precise
posture and your father's short stature,
his fierce concentration.

I tell you none of that.

Tonight I see you owning
the brow of that hill, boots planted square,
hands flying in perfect rhythm, ruling
the fire's dance as it flickers your face.

You arc your neck, mouth opening
– my God! – I did not know you
had learned do that.

And I know many things.

You do not see me – it is best.

Your mother left a trail of banana skins,
then a child; you are juggling
your own punch-line,
breathing new flames.

Every girl needs a hobby

Not needed during the show, I ooze
into his van, breathe in sweated
onions, and strip my t-shirt and bra.

He scrapes congealed pink
from the candyfloss machine
– it's all in the wrist –

wipes Whippy and ketchup
from the counter, all fresh
for intermission. I unzip

my jeans, tug at the dirty
apron strings bobbing
with his arse,

pull both his hands back
from the running tap,

slap them sticky to my skin.

He's something to do.

The same every town. I know
him well, even though the body
is always different.

Everybody leaves so why haven't I?

When I was a kid I used to love to watch the Big Top deflate,
fall in on itself in another soggy field. I would help
coax nervy ponies into the dark of their boxes
with Polo mints and muzzle nuzzling.

Then, when everything was loaded, I'd clamber
into the van or truck of whoever I felt like riding with
just before our convoy hit the road.

I don't remember anyone checking where I was.

A new town was always there for me to be loosed
on with a kaleidoscope of posters and flyers to foist
on corner shop owners, one hand behind my back,
wrist-deep in their pic 'n' mix.

A new town. But new in a boring way,
like new school uniform and bus timetables.

People leaving on their own was more interesting;
to cabarets in Blackpool, burlesque clubs in Birmingham,
to run yoga and meditation retreats in Rhyl.
Even a secure psychiatric unit.

Now I'm twenty-two years old and I still love
to see that flea-bitten tent come down, exhausted
and grubby, like so much dirty linen in the mud.

How proud The Ring Master is when he pitches
it in the next nowhere town – I don't bother
watching it go up anymore.

Kelly

S'pose I best not say you've grown; not that you've
turned out tall, eh? Didn't get my legs! It's shit

they don't let you smoke in pubs these days;
yeah, yeah, supposed to be giving up – don't you
look at me like that. When did you get all moral?

Ok – so I never sang you rock-a-byes, told you
Mummy would always be there.
Didn't lie to you, did I?

These vape things aren't up to much.
Cherry Haze, I ask you! Like huffing Airwick.

Barman where I was hostessing, Jed – proper fit,
twenty-six – I've still got it – and these young lads,
they like a bit of experience. He was

pretty, but a bit of a tit when it came to it –
thought he was, like, mystical or whatever.
All yoga and tantric sex – dead dull, that.

But anyway, he told me some old proverb,
African or something, says it takes a village
to raise a child. Course, I'd never heard

that before, but realised I knew it anyway,
cos whilst I'm not one for poncy words,
well, I'm not daft, am I? Was a village,

of sorts, eh? And the kid pissing and bawling –
you, that was. I let them get on with the raising.

No skin off my nose – they wanted to – better
for you than some foster home. I was still
around – wasn't I? Wasn't I?

Looks of it, they did a better job than I would've.
Mostly. I mean, no one taught you about hair dye.
Fucksake – you're ginger as a tomcat's arse.

And I'm here, for now. Sun, sand and sangria gets old;
no matter their begging, only so many toy boys
a woman can be fucked to suck off.

Jed? Oh, there was some student from Stuttgart.
Seventeen. Steffi has the most beautiful chakras,
the perfect downward dog at dawn.
No tits to speak of.

And then there's my knees. It happens
when you've been dancing in five inch heels
since thirteen. Least your foot got you out of that:

no one expected you to be a pretty girl on a pony,
no Ring Master was going to notice you.

Get your mum another drink, eh?

Swansong

1.   Lucky

I bring grapes and her favourite CDs,
then worry it's cruel to play Swan Lake
and Coppélia to a strapped-down ballerina.

One foot and leg is plastered to the hip and hoisted high,
the other leg a tiny straight line under the blanket;
even unconscious, these toes are *en pointe*,
an accusatory arrow to the notes
hooked at the end of the bed.

The doctors said it was a clean break,
she'd been lucky – as lucky as a snapped
high wire on opening night can ever be.
But that she'd need to stay in a while.

Her arms are winged out from her body,
hands just so on the bedrails, poised to spring
free of these pulleys and drips and grab me,
spin us on this easy-wipe floor, spin
through every set of automatic doors.

She has always been the only one
who would make me get up and dance.

2.   Less so

I'd drag him into a storage cupboard and fuck him silly
on any other day – he's cute, this doctor; innocent-looking,
which generally means he's utter filth.

He tells us about the infection that's creeping through Bella;
the drugs – that aren't working – the other drugs – that may
not work either – and she flickers her eyelids at me,
bored, and I can tell she's still pissed off she's not

allowed her make up in here. Everywhere is sanitiser
and no lipstick, certainly no germ-riddled mascara wands.

I tune out and watch the doctor's lips. He'll have dimples
when he smiles. We'll neither of us see them, I'm guessing.

3.   5:43, Maple Ward

Who are you?

It's me, it's me – I'm here.

Yes, yes – I know you are. But, Who. Are. You?

Her words – crushed tissue paper– prod
me in time with the monitors' bips.

She indicates the locker. *My handbag.*

It's empty, I tell her. *They had me take
your stuff out so no one could nick it.*

Fingers straight to a hidden pocket,
she huffs me wrong,

has me hold out my palm, then folds
my fingers hard around a metallic bite
I've known all my life.

*If you don't know who, my sweet, it's time
you went and found out.*

*I'm going soon myself.
Don't linger, now.*

I'm in the car park before I can open my fist;
the campervan keys have broken
the skin inside my hand,
crossing my palm with blood.

His name is Wayne

I never knew that. And it's not a cool
Wayne like a surname to 'John'.

My father is called Wayne.
He wears a red coat, waves his arms
and shouts at animals and humans,
humans like animals and animals
like less,

because he is more than *Wayne*
in that Ring, in that frayed old tent
with his whip;

under those lights that blast
the threadbare from his red tailcoat,
shine the sweat on his brow to magic.

The popstar mic by his mouth amplifies
his commands to bring them all on.

The Lion-Tamer! The Elephants! (Not Steve.)
The Strong Man! The Human Cannonball!

The Clowns! (Minus the annoying one
people loved so much – a lost cause.)

(And no more Amazing Bearded Ballerina
to spin, spin, pirouette, and spin!)

The Ponies! And The Stunning Dancing Girls!
(Some so young, so very, very young.)

Here in the wings, feet planted in sawdust,
my throat is raw for these matches' spent taste,
their fire with the cheap booze.
The bananas are cradled to my chest.

So much is flammable.

Daddy, notice me. But not like that.
Tonight I am making my debut.

Bringing the house down

It doesn't matter that I perform to a fast-emptying tent –
the look on The Ring Master's face is all I need;
it would do if I had no accelerant.

And I am running – well, yes – *rings* around him;
my arms fast, my hands faster, bouncing sure
on my mismatched feet to catch, ignite, launch
each righteous, fearsome flame.
I am the dancing animal
daughter he'd have coped with,
only not in a glittered bikini.

Over-ripe bananas and Lidl vodka;
my mother's favourite things brought together
with a twist, like one of those birthday cocktails
with little fireworks puttering,

only much, much bigger.

A curse-circle of seared yellow fruit traps
him at the epicentre of his kingdom.
This is my final match – I scrape its naughty
end across the box, watch it bloom blue-yellow-gold,
shiver in air that tastes like the first man I ever fucked.

I lift the lit match up between us, a nightlight
for every scared young girl who never
asked for one or it.

There is no dramatic music, no gasping crowd.
No light reflects from his eyes.

We both watch the tiny flame lick
down towards my fingers.

Please don't worry: I've made sure every single one
of his animals – even the elephants – are well away

by the time I stroke

that lit match to the canvas of my father's Big Top
with him hypnotised motionless at the centre of it.

Every family is different – reprise

There's a particular lopsided stone cottage in south Devon,
a kiln and a tortoiseshell cat come with the rental. My friend
Jolyon has an arrangement with a Totnes gift shop - tourists
go mad for his tiny clay creatures – hand-sculpted,
painted and glazed right here.

I bring him mugs of strong coffee as he works, perfectly
plucked eyebrows arched vainly away from the new
reading glasses he hates, hands dextrous as ever.

Dozens of beasts march the length of the workbench:
lions and tigers roar their jaws skyward; monkeys
wiggle their bums; bears beat bongos; ponies
with braided tails and flying legs dance.

Cream scone magnets – another moneyspinner –
dot postcards to the fridge. Lately all from Amsterdam;
and one Polaroid – her and Jozef, both crinkle-eyed
and smiling in their coffee shop doorway. A woman
who never talked of home has tumbled into one.

Jolyon and I often toast her with our mugs,
pretending to each other we're being ironic.

Lately he's started a new line.

Watchful foxes; fawns with thoughtful eyes;
hares with gymnastic haunches poised to launch;
swans with elegant feathers, as delicately strong
as ballerinas at Covent Garden.

The becoming of Lady Flambé

I leave my friend's cottage before dawn;
neither of us like goodbyes.

The van is now painted the most degenerate
orange – like my hair – with added screams
of red, yellow, gold and black flaming
every panel. Each side blazes:

Lady Flambé – this witch burns her own way!

I'm parked up and unloaded at Glastonbury
– my first – before I find it: a palm-small thing,
tucked shy in the pocket of my leather jacket.

The wrapping is rough and careless,
kitchen towel with blue flowers, clodded
with a silly amount of Sellotape.

It takes a while to fight my way in –
I sit on the van's open back; can hear music
from at least three different directions; smell
onions frying, falafels, toffee apples,
suncream, weed, and musk.

Legs stretched out – both feet bare
to the grass, the *normal* and the *other*.
People everywhere, people are smiling.

The tiny clay elephant tumbles loose
to my hand while I'm smirking badness
over those fried onions. A notch on its back
is threaded with a thin bootlace.

The creature is a small, warm weight
between my breasts as I gather
the tools of my trade:
matches, torches, accelerant, bananas.

I have everything I need to begin.

Indigo Dreams Publishing Ltd
24, Forest Houses
Cookworthy Moor
Halwill
Beaworthy
Devon
EX21 5UU
www.indigodreams.co.uk